BTS

ARMY HANDBOOK

WRITTEN BY NIKI SMITH

DESIGNED BY JON DALRYMPLE

A Pillar Box Red Publication

©2018. Published by Pillar Box Red Publishing Ltd.

ISBN 978-1-912456-21-5

Images © Getty Images

KT-478-450

£8.99

CONTENTS

BTS CHEAT SHEET 6

FAST FACTS 7

BTS PROFILES 8-14

DEBUT 15

BEGINNINGS 16-19

K-POP 20-21

K-POP BAND POSITIONS 22-23

A.R.M.Y 24-25

BTS DISCOGRAPHY 26-27

MAKING GLOBAL WAVES 29

BIG QUIZ 30

AWARDS TIME 31

KINGS OF SOCIAL MEDIA 32

BTS ON TOUR 33

SOUTH KOREA CHEAT SHEET 34

CROSSWORD 35

COLLABORATIONS 36

DANCE AND CHOREOGRAPHY 37

HIP HOP 38-39

THE BTS A-Z 40-41

WHAT DOES THE FUTURE HOLD 42

BTS GLOSSARY 43

ANSWERS 44-45

BTS CHEAT SHEET

RM, Jin, Suga, J-Hope, Jimin, V, Jungkook…

These guys have got it all: they've got the moves, the style, the talent and, most importantly of all, they've got A.R.M.Y.

Originally formed by Big Hit Entertainment through an audition process that ran between 2010 and 2012, the 7 members of the band came together as BTS in 2013.

When BTS arrived on the scene they did so in style… they picked up heaps of best newcomer/new artist awards and hit the ground running with their first single, No More Dream from their album, 2 Cool 4 Skool.

Within just four years, they had picked up more awards, accolades, and record breaking feats than anyone would think possible.

They had cycled through three eras of their look with the Skool, The Most Beautiful Moment in Life, and Wings phases, and had gained a seriously loyal and dedicated band of fans known as A.R.M.Y.

BTS are known for their catchy tunes, outstanding dance moves and their love for their fans.

There is some key vocab you'll need to pick up if you really want to prove your superfan status. The first thing is to work out your bias. Who is your favourite member of BTS? This is your guy – your bias.

You also need to know about Stan… stan means looking up to your idol and fans say they 'stan' a group. We stan BTS!

You also need to stay tuned to YouTube and subscribe to Bangtan Bombs and the V-Live app so you can really get to know the boys of BTS. Also, look out for cute memes and get ready for some serious fandom community.

But of course, if you want to know more about the boys of BTS, you'll have to read on…

Fast Facts

- BTS stands for the Bangtan Sonyeodan or Beyond the Scene

- Also known as Bulletproof Boy Scouts, and Bulletproof Boys

- They hail from South Korea

- Didn't start globally promoting until 2017 - 2013 was Korean debut

- There are 7 members of the band

- Three members are talented rappers

- They produce most of their own music

- They did not know each other before they were formed by Big Hit Entertainment

- Hip hop is a big inspiration

- They have LOYAL fans known as BTS ARMY

- They are kings of social media

Suga

Name:
Min Yoon Gi

Solo name:
Agust D

Position:
Rapper, Producer

Birthday: 9th March, 1993
Star Sign: Pisces
Hometown: Daegu, South Korea
Weight: 59 kg **Height:** 174cm
Lucky Number: 3
Favourite Colour: White
Favourite Food: Meat
Hobbies: Basketball, relaxing, photography, avoiding work
Role Models: Kanye West, Lupe Fiasco, Lil Wayne, Hit boy
Personality Type: Careful, calm, passionate
Secret Fact: He bites his nails

Jung Ho Seok

Name:
Jung Ho Seok

Position:
Rapper, Dancer

Birthday: 18th February, 1994
Star Sign: Aquarius
Hometown: Gwangju, South Korea
Languages: Korean, Japanese, English
Weight: 65kg   **Height:** 177cm
Lucky Number: 7
Favourite Food: Kimchi
Hobbies: Listening to music, window shopping
Nickname: The BTS 'Mother'
Role Models: A$AP Rocky, J.Cole, G-Dragon
Personality Type: Problem solver, mischievous, friendly
Secret Fact: He sleeps with both arms above his head

Rap Monster

Name:
Kim Nam Joon

Position:
Rapper, Leader

Birthday: 12th September, 1994
Star Sign: Virgo
Hometown: Ilsan-gu, Goyang,
Seoul, South Korea
Languages: Korean, English
(taught himself by
watching Friends!)
Weight: 67kg **Height:** 181cm
Lucky Number: 1
Favourite Colour: Black
Favourite Food: Meat,
Korean noodles
Hobbies: Surfing the internet
Role Models: Kanye West, A$AP
Secret Fact: Studied in New Zealand

Jimin

Name:

Park Jimin

Position:

Vocalist, Dancer

Birthday: 13th October, 1995
Star Sign: Libra
Hometown: Geumjeong District, Busan, South Korea
Weight: 61kg Height: 173cm
Lucky Number: 3
Favourite Colour: Blue and black
Favourite Food: Pork, duck, chicken, fruit, kimchi
Hobbies: Relaxing
Role Model: Taeyang from BIGBANG
Secret Fact: His childhood dream was to be a police officer!

V

Name:
Kim Tae Hyung

Position:
Vocalist, Visual

Birthday: 30th December, 1995
Star Sign: Capricorn
Hometown: Seo District, Daegu, South Korea
Weight: 62kg
Height: 178cm
Lucky Number: 10
Favourite Colour: Black, green and white
Favourite Food: Japchae, meat
Role Model: His dad
Secret Fact: He collects big dolls

Jungkook

Name:
Jeon Jeong-Guk

Position:
Centre and Maknae

Birthday: 1st September, 1997
Star Sign: Virgo
Hometown: Mandeok-dong, Busan, South Korea
Weight: 66kg **Height:** 178cm
Lucky Number: 1
Favourite Colour: Black, white and red
Hobbies: Drawing
Role Model: G-Dragon from BIGBANG
Secret Fact: He forgets to respond to texts!

13

Jin

Name:
Kim Seok Jin

Position:
Vocalist, Visual

Birthday: 4th December, 1992
Star Sign: Sagittarius
Hometown: Gwacheon, Gyeonggi-do, South Korea
Languages: Korean, Japanese, English
Weight: 63kg
Height: 179cm
Favourite Colour: Pink
Favourite Food: Lobster, chicken, burgers, pizza, Korean noodles
Hobbies: Cooking, video games, anime
Personality Type: Hardworking, carefree, responsible
Secret Fact: He wears glasses and can't handle scary movies

DEBUT

BTS burst onto the world music scene in 2013 when they released their first single, 'No More Dream'.

The day of their debut is hotly contested date amongst ARMY; was it the 12th or the 13th June?

The first album is 2 Cool 4 Skool and was released at the same time. The band also released We Are Bulletproof Pt. 2.

BTS celebrate their debut anniversary every year.

Their first single won them a number of awards including Best Newcomer Award at the Melon Music Awards, and a Rookie Award at The Golden Disc awards in 2014.

Big Hit Entertainment teased the forthcoming release of an unknown debut album with a countdown timer on their webpage.

BTS made an instant impact and made it onto the Billboard World Digital Songs chart rising to 14th by the end of June that year.

On their debut, BTS rocked a pretty edgy look consisting of heavy eye make-up, black hip hop clothing, leather jackets, basketball jerseys, and heavy chains around their necks.

BEGIN

The first five years of BTS' career have been a wild ride. With overwhelming successes, more awards than they can handle, and millions of loyal fans all over the world, the boys of BTS have every right to feel a little overwhelmed with their incredible success. So just how did it all begin?

BTS had their first TV show, called *Rookie King* in September 2013. At the same time, they released their first single: N.O and their first mini album: *O!RUL8,2?*

By November of 2013, they had won their first award for Best New Artists at the Melon Music Awards.

<<<<<<< 2014 >>>>>>>

After a stellar rise following their debut, 2014 got off to a great start with the band winning Rookie of the Year at the 28th Golden Disk Awards on the 1st January 2014.

By February, momentum really started to build for the band when they released *Boy in Luv* and won New Artist of the Year at the 3rd Gaon Chart K-pop Awards. If that wasn't enough, February also saw BTS release their second mini album, *Skool Luv Affair*, which entered in at number 3 on the Billboard World Album chart. Impressive!

April saw the release of the *Just One Day* music video and the boys made their Japanese debut with *Wake Up*.

July of that year saw the band appear in their TV show, *American Hustle Life* which told the story of their first trip to America. They performed *Oh Happy Day* at their *Show and Prove* concert.

August of 2014 saw the band attend KCON LA, release the Danger music video, and their first full length album *Dark and Wild*.

NINGS

THE STORY SO FAR...

September they launch their webtoon series, *Hip Hop Monster*. In October 2014, the band released their *War of Hormone* music video and at the end of the year in December, BTS made their first appearance at Mnet Asian Music Awards.

<<<<<<< 2015 >>>>>>>

January of 2015 saw the 29th Golden Disk Awards where the band picked up a Bonsang Award. They also attended the 25th Seoul Music awards where they were presented with a New Artists award.

February saw the boys heading off on their first Japanese tour, *Wake Up: Open Your Eyes*.

By March of 2015, collaborations with western artists began and the band released *P.D.D Please Don't Die* with Warren G. They also set off on their first world tour: *2015 Live Trilogy Episode II: The Red Bullet*.

April saw the release of the *I Need U* music vid and the band's 3rd mini album *The Most Beautiful Moment in Life Pt. 1*.

June saw the release of the first Japanese single *For You*, and then the release of the *Dope* music video which hit number 3 on Billboard's World Digital chart.

November saw BTS win Best Dance Male at Melon Music Awards and release the Run music video as well as their fourth mini album, *The Most Beautiful Moment in Life Pt.2*.

By December, the boys of BTS won Best World Performer at the Mnet Asian Music awards.

<<<<<<< 2016 >>>>>>>

January 2016 started off strong for BTS with another Bonsang Award win at both the Seoul Music Awards and the Golden Disk Awards.

February sees them win a World Pop Star Award at the 5th Gaon Chart K-Pop Awards.

Spring of 2016 saw the band release the Young Forever music video, Followed in May by the release of music videos for *Fire and Save Me*.

In June, the band headline at KCON LA and follow this with a further headline appearance in July at KCON, New York city.

October saw the band release *Blood Sweat & Tears* along with the music video which achieves the band's first 'all kill'.

In the same month they also released their second full length album, *Wings* which hit number one on World Digital Songs chart and helped the band to win a Cultural Minister award at Korean Pop Culture and Arts Awards.

In November the Wings tour sells out and extra dates are added. The band also win their first Daesang for Best Album of the Year at Melon Music Awards which was a very BIG DEAL!

December closes out the year positively with another win at the Mnet Asian Music awards for Artist of the Year.

<<<<<<< 2017 >>>>>>>

Another year, another great start for the boys of BTS. January 2017 kicks off with winning the Global K-Pop Artists Award at the 31st Golden Disk Awards, as well as Bonsang awards at the 26th Seoul Music Awards.

February saw the band ranking 5th on the Forbes Korea Power Celebrity chart (in first place was Park Bogum, second was Song Joongki, third was Twice, and in fourth place was EXO). BTS also release the *Spring Day* and *Not Today* music videos and they win album of the year for *You Never Walk Alone* at the 6th Gaon K-Pop Chart Awards.

In March, Rap Monster teamed up with rapper, Wale and released his first solo venture, *Change* to critical acclaim.

Billboard Hot 100 – the first K-pop band to do so. And if that still wasn't enough, they then hit the Billboard 200 – again, the first K-pop band to achieve this. A big year for the boys!

<<<<<<< 2018 >>>>>>>

After all their successes, 2018 kicked off in style for BTS with the announcement that the band would perform at the Billboard Music Awards. During the performance, the band debuted their new single from the *Love Yourself 'Tear'* album and proved they were leaders when it comes to riding the Korean wave. 2018 sees the band embark on a huge tour taking in Seoul, LA, Texas, Canada, Newark, Chicago, London, Amsterdam, Berlin and Paris.

May saw BTS win the Top Social Artist Award at the Billboard Music awards, and in July they won the Artist Award at Korean Broadcasting Awards.

September saw the release of the band's fifth mini album, *Love Yourself 'Tear'* and the *DNA* music vid.

September proved to be a game-changer for the band as Love Yourself 'Tear' became the first K-pop album to be sold on Amazon and DNA became the first K-pop group single to hit the US iTunes top ten coming in at number 4. The video for the track became the 11th most viewed video of all time in the first 24 hours.

If that wasn't enough, BTS became the first Korean artists to enter Spotify's Global top 50 chart. They held their first ever comeback showcase which was live-streamed worldwide (and featured the infamous

K-pop, or Korean pop, is a crazily popular genre of music that has burst onto the scene in recent years. Characterised by groups of artists, mega choreography, and a huge variety of innovative audio-visual elements, a K-pop concert is really something to be seen!

While it's hard to define K-pop musically given that artists draw inspiration from all sorts of Western musical styles, what is for sure, is that K-pop is the hottest music around.

For a K-pop band, anything goes: hip hop, jazz, gospel, classical music, reggae, EDM, and traditional Korean music all find their way into the latest K-pop hits.

According to those in the know, the K-pop movement began in 1992 with the huge Korean band, Seo Taiji and Boys. These guys are credited with transforming modern Korean music into the K-pop we know and love today.

Things really kicked off with K-pop idol culture in 1996, with the crazily successful boy band, H.O.T. But what exactly is a K-pop idol?

K-POP IDOLS

K-pop idols are created after a complex series of mass auditions (closed, or public), or sometimes even street casting, run by huge entertainment companies. Street casting, or scouting, is often based on looks alone and is all down to luck.

Successful potentials go on to become a trainee in a kind of apprenticeship that can last months or even years. During their apprenticeship, trainees are schooled in dance, vocals, and language. Trainees can be very young and some of them even combine their trainee classes with regular school!

This method of finding the next generation of K-pop stars was created by Lee Soo-Man, the founder of S.M. Entertainment one of the originators of the K-pop movement.

The cost of transforming just one trainee into a K-pop star can run into millions of dollars.

SUPER FANS

K-pop is characterised by legions of super fans made up of teens and young adults. Largely thanks to social media, huge marketing campaigns and the power of Korean television, K-pop has become a force to be reckoned with, not just in Korea and surrounding countries, but also around the world. The global spread of K-pop and other Korean youth cultures is known as the Korean Wave.

SOUND AND VISION

A big feature of K-pop is the focus of the genre on audio-visual performance and content. This means that K-pop concerts are a spectacular blend of amazing choreography, sharply dressed stars, catchy cross-genre songs, and exciting video elements too.

ENGLISH

Many K-pop songs have English phrases or are even entirely written in English. This helps to spread the power of K-pop around the world as English is so commonly spoken. A happy side effect of this is that many Western music stars have also been involved in the production of K-pop tracks for big idols. Artists such as Akon, Snoop Dog, and Kanye West have all been featured on K-pop tracks.

DANCING

One unique feature of K-pop is the outstanding choreography. Many K-pop artists work in big groups (just like BTS) and so concerts will often see members of the band switching positions according to who is singing, or routines that take advantage of having many people involved.

K-pop dance moves are tough – no wonder it takes years of training to become an idol!

Another factor is the 'point-dance'. Point moves are often repeated several times during a track and can be considered as the signature moves in a song. Point moves also often reflect the main theme of the songs.

K-pop choreography is so popular that there are dedicated K-pop dance troupes all over the world and tutorials all over the internet!

FASHION

K-pop is big on fashion. Stars are often described as muses for big clothing brands and fashion trends amongst the youth of Korea are often originate from K-pop stars.

Because K-pop makes the most of lots of different styles of music, there is lots of diversity in clothing styles. Streetwear, the retro look, and futurism are just some of the styles that can be seen in any K-pop video.

HALLYU WAVE

Korea is really proud of its most successful export – K-pop! The movement is so well supported that even the government's Ministry of Culture is involved in trying to spread the word and influence of K-pop. Global fans are even invited to Korea to the annual K-Pop World Festival.

K-POP

THE LEADER: The leader of a K-pop band is often the oldest member and is supposed to motivate and look after the other members of the band. The leader is likely to be the one who accepts awards, and gives speeches. RM is the leader of BTS (as well as the rapper).

THE RAPPERS: These are the guys responsible for the rapping sections of K-pop songs. There are usually three rappers: the main rapper (the best one who will also write his own lyrics), the lead rapper (the second best who usually begins the rapping section), and the sub-rapper (the third best). RM (Rap Monster) is the main rapper of BTS, and Suga is the lead. J-Hope is also a rapper.

THE VOCALIST: Most K-pop groups have a number of specialist vocalists consisting of the main vocalist (the best one who gets the most demanding vocal parts), the lead vocalist (the second best who often sings the chorus), and the sub-vocalist (who supports the main and lead and gets fewer singing lines). Jungkook and Jin are the vocalists in BTS, and Suga and J-Hope are the leads.

THE DANCERS: As the name suggests, the dancers are the best dancers of the group and there is usually a main dancer (the best), and a lead dancer (the second best). The main dancer in BTS is J-Hope and Jimin, and the lead is V.

BAND POSITIONS

THE VISUALS: The visual is the best looking member of the group and can be the leader. In BTS, this role is taken by Jin and V.

THE FACE OF THE GROUP: Not to be confused with the visual, the face of the group is the most popular member and has a specific job to do and that is to bring attention to the group. The face serves as a representative of the band and represents them in interviews, or other public events like awards shows.

THE CENTRE: The centre of a K-pop group is usually positioned in the middle for photoshoots, concerts and Performances. They might be the most popular, or the most talented dancer. In BTS the centre is Jungkook.

THE MAKNAE: The Maknae is the youngest member of the group and is usually associated with being cute, shy, and adorable. The BTS maknae is Jungkook.

A.R.M.Y

K-pop fans are serious. Legions of totally devoted young women who spend serious amounts of time, energy and money on supporting and following their idols are the lifeblood of the K-pop business.

Most groups have their own dedicated fan clubs and these are often given an identifying name, and a group colour. Fan clubs are involved in charitable works as well with fan rice providing much needed rice for those in need.

K-pop fans have a social conscience and aim to be seen as mature and responsible.

Fan rice are stacks of rice bags highly decorated with images and ribbons in the fan club colours. The bags are donated to the band and are then donated to charities of the band's choosing.

In South Korea, there are couriers who ship rice directly to concert venues from farms. Another way to show their appreciation is for fans to buy lunches for their idols while they are on tour.

There is also the famous K-pop fanchant: whenever there is a new release, fans chant band member's names during concerts in the sections where there is no singing.

In the case of BTS, fans are known by the acronym, A.R.M.Y which stands for Adorable Representative MC for Youth, and the club colour is silver grey with official silver grey light sticks used at concerts and other performances.

The A.R.M.Y have three fanchants with which to vocalise their support for BTS: the first and most frequently heard, is when fans chant the full names of the band members followed by a shout of BTS in this order:

Kim Namjoon! Kim Seokjin! Min Yoongi! Jung Hoseok! Park Jimin! Kim Taehyung! Jeon Jeongguk! BTS!

The second is when fans simply chant BTS! Repeatedly and is most commonly heard for particular songs such as DNA and Fire.

The third type of BTS fanchant comes when fans echo certain words of songs as the band sing them – there are loads of tutorials and cheat sheets online that fans consult to make themselves fanchanting experts.

A.R.M.Y

A.R.M.Y have some serious fan power. Members are devoted, loyal, and possess superior social media power giving their band more re-tweets than Kanye West and Justin Bieber.

Global fan support for the BTS boys meant their album WINGS was the most successful K-pop album of 2010 in South

Korea ever. It even charted on the American Billboard 200 twice in a row, as well as making it to number 62 on the UK album chart - this is seriously impressive stuff for a band from South Korea.

While every K-pop band has its own loyal band of fans, there seems to be something special between BTS and A.R.M.Y. The relationship between the band and their fans is so strong that the boys even wrote several special songs for their fans, including 'Two! Three! (To Many More Good Days)'.

Fandom feuds

With such loyal fans and so many K-pop bands out there, it's no wonder that feelings get a little heated from time to time. In an effort to calm a spiralling fan feud situation, the boys of BTS wrote to the fandoms of other K-pop groups in an effort to calm things down. This shows us that not only are ARMY loyal and dedicated to the boys of BTS, but that BTS are just as loyal and dedicated to their fans.

Both fans and BTS can be described as the most awesome, genuine and passionate K-pop ambassadors.

ARMY also show their support for BTS by writing their own songs, making videos, writing fiction stories, and drawing their own fan art about their favourite band. Some of their biggest local campaigns are for billboards that celebrate significant events like band member's birthdays or a comeback. Other fan projects include making Facebook pages, designing huge banners, or running fan web groups online - this is seriously one dedicated bunch!

There are branches of ARMY all over the world with K-ARMY (Korea) spreading the love and the positive messages of BTS.

In fact, the K-ARMY are responsible for making a Stanford Professor, James R. Doty's little-known book, Into the Magic Shop number one on the Korean book charts. Fans rushed to buy it after it was mentioned in Magic Shop, one of the tracks form the album, Love Yourself: Tear - now that's fan power!

BTS DISC

KOREAN STUDIO ALBUMS

Dark and Wild

The debut studio album of BTS, released 2014. The title track is Danger, and War of Hormone was promoted as the second track. Peaked at number 2 on the Gaon Album Chart, and number 3 on the US Billboard World Albums Chart.

<<<<<<<<<<<<< Track listing >>>>>>>>>>>>>

- ▶ Intro: What Am I To You?
- ▶ Danger
- ▶ War of Hormone
- ▶ Hip Hop Lover
- ▶ Let Me Know
- ▶ Rain
- ▶ BTS Cypher Pt. 3 Killer
- ▶ Interlude: What Are You doing?
- ▶ Would You Turn Off Your Cellphone
- ▶ Blanket Kick
- ▶ 24/7=Heaven
- ▶ Look Here
- ▶ 2ND Grade
- ▶ Outro: Does This Make Sense?

Wings

Released 2016, influenced by the coming of age story of Hermann Hesse and explores the themes of temptation and growth. BTS's second studio album hit number 1 on both the Gaon and US Billboard 200 charts.

<<<<<<<<<<<<< Track listing >>>>>>>>>>>>>

- ▶ Intro: Boy Meets Evil
- ▶ Blood Sweat and Tears
- ▶ Begin
- ▶ Lie
- ▶ Stigma
- ▶ First Love
- ▶ Reflection
- ▶ MAMA
- ▶ Awake
- ▶ Lost
- ▶ BTS Cypher 4
- ▶ Am I Wrong
- ▶ 21st Century Girl
- ▶ 2!3!
- ▶ Interlude: Wings

Love Yourself: Tear

Released in 2018, this is the third studio album for the boys of BTS. Fake Love is the lead single and the album reached number 1 on the Gaon chart as well as number 1 on the US Billboard 200, and number 8 on the UK chart.

<<<<<<<<<<<<< Track listing >>>>>>>>>>>>>

- ▶ Intro: Singularity
- ▶ Fake Love
- ▶ The Truth Untold
- ▶ 134340
- ▶ Paradise
- ▶ Love Maze
- ▶ Magic Shop
- ▶ Airplane pt. 2
- ▶ Anpanman
- ▶ So What
- ▶ Outro: Tear

OGRAPHY

MINI ALBUMS

O!RUL8,2?

The 1st BTS mini-album released in 2013 containing 10 new tracks with N.O as the lead single.

Skool Luv Affair, 2014

The 2nd mini-album and the third in the Skool trilogy. Released in 2014, another ten new tracks many dealing with social issues.

The Most Beautiful Moment in Life, Part 1

Released in 2015, this is the 3rd mini-album for the band with 9 new tracks. This album features the crazily successful single, Dope and a new musical direction for the band.

The Most Beautiful Moment in Life, Part 2

The 4th mini-album, this was another 9 tracks also released in 2015. This mini album was released in two versions and the lead track is Run.

Love Yourself: Her

The 5th mini album released in 2017, in four different versions. The lead track is DNA.

The band have also released three

JAPANESE STUDIO ALBUMS:

Wake Up

Youth

Face Yourself

COMPILATION ALBUMS

2 Cool 4 Skool / O!RUL8,2?

The Best of Bodan Shonendan - Japan Edition

The Most Beautiful Moment in Life: Young Forever

The Best of Bodan Shonendan - Korea edition

REPACKAGED ALBUMS:

BTS have also released two special albums that are thematic continuations of previous albums. You Never Walk Alone, for example, is a continuation of Wings and Young Forever is the continuation of The Two Most Beautiful Moments in Life albums.

You Never Walk Alone additional tracks:
▶ Spring Day
▶ Not Today
▶ Outro: Wings
▶ A Supplementary Story: You Never Walk Alone

Skool Luv Affair Special Addition tracks:
▶ Miss Right
▶ I Like It (Slow Jam Remix)

BTS

MAKING GLOBAL WAVES

The Korean Wave is the phenomena lead by K-pop bands that spreads Korean culture and music across the globe. One thing is for sure, the boys from BTS are surfing a huge wave of their own making right now.

- They were the first K-pop band to perform at a US television awards show when they performed at the AMAs in 2017.

- They are the first K-pop band to be nominated for and win a Billboard Music Award.

- They are the first K-pop band to go Gold with MIC Drop (Remix)

- The have sold the most copies of any album on South Korea's Gaon chart with Love Yourself, Tear.

- They made iTunes history by topping national iTunes charts in a whopping 73 regions with mini album, Love Yourself 'Tear'.

- The title track DNA came first in 29 iTunes regions

- DNA got to number 4 in the iTunes music video charts.

- DNA also broke the record for the fastest K-pop music video to reach 10 million views on YouTube.

- They are the first K-pop band to hit 50 million listens on Spotify.

- They have the record for the highest ranked K-pop track on Spotify's Global Viral 50 chart.

BIG QUIZ

re the rappers in BTS?

year did BTS make their
t?

the member of the band who
oys photography?

ch two members of the band
ve a December birthday?

o taught himself English by
atching Friends?

ho sleeps with both arms above
is head?

Which member of the band
collects big dolls?

When was V born?

What was the name of their first
Japanese tour?

What was the name of the single
that achieved the band's first
All-Kill?

- ☐ Who was the rapper who teamed up with RM on Change?

- ☐ Who is the maknae of BTS?

- ☐ What year did the band win Choice International Artists at the Teen Choice Awards?

- ☐ What is the name of the band's 2018 tour?

- ☐ What does hallyu mean?

- ☐ Who is the centre of BTS?

- ☐ What does A.R.M.Y. stand for?

- ☐ Which book hit number 1 in the Korean book chart thanks to a mention in a BTS song?

- ☐ What was the name of BTS' first Japanese studio album?

- ☐ What is the lead single on O!RUL8,2?

AWARD TIME

BTS are record breakers and have amassed serious amounts of golden hardware. Ever since they hit the ground running, they won awards right from the very start picking up numerous best newcomer/best new artist awards. And they didn't stop there... through the five years following the BTS debut, these guys have picked up award after award, after award... and the ride doesn't seem to be showing any signs of stopping!

Teen Choice Awards
Choice International Artists, 2017

Nickelodeon USA Kids' Choice Award
Favourite Global Music Star 2018

MTV Europe Music Awards
Best Korean Act 2015

Billboard Music Awards
Top Social Artist, 2017, 2018

Seoul Music Awards
New Artist Award, 2014
Bonsang Award, 2015, 2016, 2017
Best Male Dance Performance Award, 2017
Record of the Year, Wings, 2017
Best Music Video Award, 2017
Daesang Award, 2018

Melon Music Awards
New Artist of the Year, 2013
Best Male Dance, 2015
Album of the Year, 2016
Top Ten Artists, 2017
Global Artist, 2017
Song of the Year, Spring Day, 2017
Music Video Award, DNA, 2017

Gaon Chart Music Award
New Artist of the Year, 2014
World Rookie Award, 2015
K-Pop World Hallyu Star Award, 2014

Golden Disk Awards
New Rising Star Award, 2014
Disk Bosang Dark and Wild, 2015
Global K-Pop Artist, 2017

Asia Artist Award
Best Icon Award, Singer, 2016
Best Icon Award, Music, 2016

KINGS OF SOCIAL MEDIA

BTS are the kings of social media. They make use of a number of channels and platforms to communicate with their fans and spread the word of any new releases, performances, concerts and tours. BTS have millions of followers across their platforms.

The Billboard social 50 measures reach across social networks and BTS have shown time and again that they really do rule the social media waves. They topped the chart for 31 weeks between 2016-2017.

They were the most retweeted artists on Twitter in 2016, they have 15.3 million Twitter followers, almost 9 million YouTube subscribers and a few million morte fans on Facebook – these numbers of climbing all the time.

So where can you find the boys of BTS?

Twitter: @bts_twt

Youtube: BangtanTV (Remember to click CC for English subtitles!)

V-Live: Where BTS host their live streams

Instagram: The boys of BTS are insta-ready!

Reality Shows: BTS Gayo and Run BTS (Check out two top rated episodes: American Hustle Life and Rookie King.)

If you really want to get to know the personalities and individual quirks of each member of the band, check out the Bangtan Bombs. These are short, goofy, cute mini-vlogs that really help the boys to express their personalities.

BTS ON TOUR

If there is one thing to know about BTS, it is that these boys are crazy busy. The life of an idol is never easy but especially not so when you are an idol in BTS. Since their debut in 2013, the band have toured South Korea, Japan, Singapore, the Philippines, Thailand, Macau, China, the United States, Germany, Sweden and Canada either with tours of their music, or in fan meet and greets.

BTS TOURS

★ ★ ★ **2014** ★ ★ ★
BTS Live Trilogy Episode II: The Red Bullet

★ ★ ★ **2015** ★ ★ ★
BTS 1ST Japan Tour Wake Up: Open Your Eyes

★ ★ ★ **2015** ★ ★ ★
BTS Live Trilogy Episode II: The Red Bullet Tour

★ ★ ★ **2015** ★ ★ ★
BTS LIVE: The Most Beautiful Moment in Life On Stage

★ ★ ★ **2016** ★ ★ ★
BTS LIVE The Most Beautiful Moment in Life On Stage: Epilogue

★ ★ ★ **2017** ★ ★ ★
BTS Live Trilogy Episode III: The Wings Tour

★ ★ ★ **And most importantly...** ★ ★ ★

BTS will embark on their latest tour in the summer of 2018:
BTS World Tour: Love Yourself

They will be performing in the UK for the first time and will play London's O2 Arena! The band were originally due to play just one date but thanks to the passion of their fans, an extra date was added.

SOUTH KOREA CHEAT SHEET

Want to know more about the country that created BTS? Here are the top facts about Korea that you need to know!

- South Korea likes to talk about poo.
- It's an old superstition that when red ink is used to write someone's name in South Korea, it means they are dead – or about to die.
- Before BTS, most people around the world were already familiar with K-Pop thanks to Psy's 2011 summer hit, Gangnam Style. This hit topped the charts of 30 countries!
- People in South Korea are big fans of cosmetic surgery with an estimated 1 in 3 women having endured a cosmetic procedure in the name of beauty.
- Group blind dates are popular in South Korea. Known as So-Getting, the practice is especially popular with university students.
- People in Seoul are a tired bunch with an average sleep per night of just 6 hours.
- Robots are already on the rise in tech-loving South Korea. They are used to guard prisons and the border with North Korea.
- South Korea's national dish is Kimchi which means South Koreans have excellent gut health.
- Ten pin bowling is crazy popular after it was introduced by American GIs in World War II.
- Cranes are good luck symbols.
- The Korean War never officially ended but a cease-fire has been upheld since the 1950s.
- Taekwondo is South Korea's most famous sport.
- The most common family names in South Korea are Lee, Park and Kim.

CROSSWORD

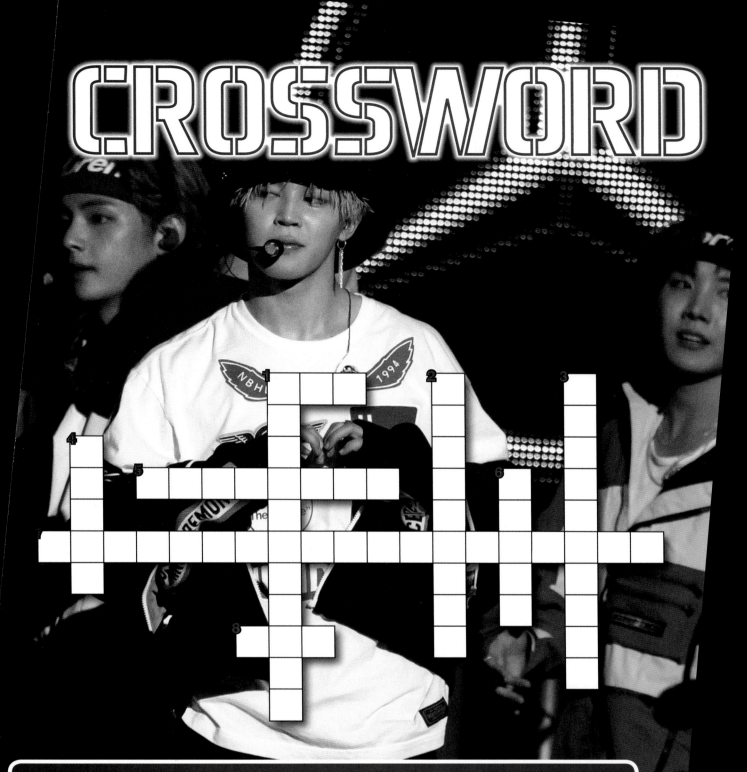

ACROSS

1 Which BTS MV has the most difficult dance routine? (3)

5 Who forgets to respond to text messages? (8)

7 Name the company that formed BTS. (3,3,13)

8 Which member of BTS secretly wears glasses? (3)

DOWN

1 Name the band's first studio album. (4,3,4)

2 Name the BTS YouTube channel. (7,2)

3 The first TV show for BTS. (6,4)

4 Which member of the band is a Libra? (5)

6 Name the second studio album. (5)

COLLABORATIONS

EVERYONE WANTS A PIECE OF BTS!

Artists from around the world want to share in the success of BTS and work with them thanks to the wide range of topics they sing about and the wide range of musical styles that they use to inspire their music.

BTS hit America - hard!

Their album *Love Yourself: Her* entered the American top ten, as did their single *DNA* - no wonder American artists are queueing up to work with the Bangtan boys!

The Chainsmokers

After meeting the boys at the Billboard Awards, The Chainsmokers collaborated on the track, *Best of Me*.

Wale

Wale caught a sneaky-peak of RM doing his thing on one of the rapper's own tracks, and he liked what he saw. Wale collaborated on RM's track Change.

Steve Aoki

Not only has Steve Aoki, wonder DJ and producer broadcast his support for the band, but he remixed their track, *MIC Drop*.

DNCE

There is a rumoured collab in the works between DNCE and BTS.

Warren G

Veteran of the hip hop world, Warren G collaborated with RM on the song *P.D.D.*

The world is BTS's oyster, with so many collabs lined up already, who knows what we might see in the future?!

DANCE AND CHOREOGRAPHY

The boys of BTS put some serious time into perfecting their crazy-skilful dance moves. The routines in their performances and videos are seriously complex!

The main dancer in BTS is J-Hope and Jimin and the lead is V. The band make use of levels and formations giving each member of the band a spotlight depending on who is singing or rapping. This technique also shines the spotlight on the band's main dancers, especially for more complicated sequences of chorography.

In *Spring Day* for example, Jin sings and walks across the stage and the other guys move with him. Similarly, in *Blood, Sweat and Tears*, there is a separation aspect as Suga raps and the others move away from him.

The point dance is also an important aspect of K-pop that the boys from BTS have mastered. The point dance is the main section of the dance routine that becomes associated with the song or concept or era. The point dance is like the trademark of a particular moment in the life of a K-pop band.

The life of a K-pop idol is physically demanding and the stars of BTS are no exception. The boys are physically incredibly fit and they have the added problem of having to remember countless dance moves – in the right order. These boys have skills!

It is the choreography of *DNA* that stands out however.

According to the boys, their choreographer, Son Sung Deuk spent sleepless nights coming up with all the moves and they freely admit that it is the hardest routine they have ever done. Son Sung Deuk was helped out by working with well-known urban dance choreographer, Keone Madrid.

DNA is also the track that displays J-Hope's excellence: while the other boys picked up the fiendishly complex routine in an amazing 4 hours, J-Hope had it licked after just 10 minutes!

The BTS boys release rehearsal videos of their dance routines and there are tons of tutorials on YouTube. Check out their channel for all their latest moves.

Hip Hop
Hip Hop
Hip Hop
Hip Hop
Hip Hop
Hip Hop
Hip Hop
Hip Hop
Hip Hop

Mainstream American Hip Hop and K-pop go way back. For many years, K-pop stars have been heavily influenced by original American hip hop both through music, fashion and visual style.

Korea has a popular, underground hip hop scene of its own and RM has often expressed his love for hip hop in interviews. The Bangtan Boys have even taken part in a reality show where they visited LA to be educated in all things hip hop.

It's no wonder then that with a band like BTS, hip hop influences come to the foreground of their music.

BTS use aspects from hip hop such as rap sections of songs, rap lyrics, references to making and spending money, urban scenes in their music videos and hip hop style clothing.

The thing is though, how did hip hop get so big and influential in Korea?

The hip hop origin story lies in African American culture in the Bronx, NYC from the late 70s onwards. The genre rose to massive popularity in the 80s and 90s but rap songs really came to global attention with the Sugar Hill Gang's Rapper's Delight in 1979.

As the genre developed, so too did global media. Channels like MTV, responsible for the rise in the popularity of music videos, were broadcast around the world – including South Korea.

American culture has always been attractive to other countries so it's no surprise that Korean youth culture latched onto the big bang made by hip hop and its amazing popularity around the world. American hip hop makes a big visual splash and this is where the real link between hip and K-pop can be found.

Hip hop combines four elements: the DJ, the rapper, graffiti, and B-boying (dancing). With this in mind, it's easy to see that BTS's rapping sections, dance moves, fashion and the importance placed on the visual experience might all have their roots in the music of hip hop.

So, RM, Suga and J-Hope use their rap skills to tell stories about hope and change through wordplay, clever lyrics and rhythm – just like their mainstream American hip hop idols.

HE BTS A-Z

All-kill – the name given to a newly released track that hits no. 1 on all of South Korea's music charts at one time

Bonsang – these are given at awards ceremonies to acknowledge outstanding music achievements

Comeback – the start of a new era in a band's career

Daesang – the grand prize awarded at annual year-end K-pop awards ceremonies

Emoji – the first K-pop emojis were released in 2016 on Twitter

Fanchant – chants sounded by fans at certain times in live concerts

Give it to Me – a track from Suga's first solo venture, *Agust D*

[H]   Hallyu – this means Korean Wave, or in other words, all Korean cultural exports

[I]   Instiz – one of the ranking systems which monitors the major music charts of South Korea

[J]   J-Hope

[K]   K-pop

[L]   Leader – this is RM!

[M]   Maknae – or the youngest person in the group, Jungkook!

[N]   Noona – this is used for males to address older females and is often used to describe ...

O   Omo! – This is the Korean version of OMG!

P   Perfect All-Kill – the name given to a track that has an All-Kill and lands at number one on the Instiz Weekly Chart

Q   Quadruple Crown – awarded after a band wins 4 awards at the same weekly music show in a row

R   Rookie – used to describe newcomers to the world of K-pop

S   Sasaeng – Sasaeng fans are too obsessed and do crazy things like breaking into hotel rooms

T   Trainee – trainees are wannabe idols in training. They undergo months, and sometimes years, of intense training in dancing, singing and performance, often after having competed in rounds of auditions

U   US Billboard – an American chart of popular music

V   V-live – an app and website where K-pop bands broadcast short videos

W   *War of Hormone* – a lead track from *Dark and Wild*

X   Xmas – the boys always release seasonal specials as a Christmas gift to fans

Y   YouTube – Come on… you know what YouTube is, right?!

Z   Zero Promotions – the track *Spring Day* entered the US Billboard Bubbling Under Hot 100 Singles chart without any promotion

WHAT DOES THE FUTURE HOLD?

WHO KNOWS WHERE THE FUTURE OF BTS LIES? WILL THEY CONTINUE TO RISE IN POPULARITY? WILL THEY CARRY ON WINNING MULTIPLE AWARDS AND TOURING THE GLOBE ON AN EVER-INCREASING SCALE?

2018 SEES THE 5TH ANNIVERSARY OF THEIR DEBUT AND THIS SHOWS THE BAND IS STILL YOUNG. THEY HAVE PLENTY MORE OPPORTUNITIES TO GROW AND DEVELOP, BUILDING THEIR CATALOGUE AND HONING THOSE DANCE SKILLS.

ONE AREA IN WHICH THE BAND CAN EASILY CONTINUE TO GROW IS IN THE WESTERN MARKET – THAT MEANS AMERICA AND EUROPE. THERE IS NO DOUBT THAT BTS HAVE DONE A LOT TO SPREAD THE WORD OF K-POP BUT THERE IS STILL PLENTY OF WORK TO BE DONE HERE. WITH JUST TWO TOUR DATES IN THE UK IN THE PIPELINE, MANY OF THOSE IN THE KNOW PREDICT A EUROPEAN TOUR WITH LOTS OF ADDED DATES.

SO, CONTINUING TO ADD TO THE DIVERSITY OF MAINSTREAM MUSIC, BREAKING WESTERN MUSIC RECORDS AND CONTINUING TO RAISE AWARENESS OF THE K-POP VIBE ALL SEEM LIKE POSITIVE MOVES IN THE RIGHT DIRECTION FOR THE BOYS FROM SOUTH KOREA.

AND WHAT ABOUT SOLO ENDEAVOURS?

SUGA AND RM HAVE ALREADY HAD SOLO SUCCESSES AWAY FROM THE BAND AND HAVE COLLABORATED WITH OTHER ARTISTS. PERHAPS BTS WILL SEE MORE SPOTLIGHTS SHONE ON THEIR VARIOUS SOLO EFFORTS?

WHATEVER THE FUTURE MAY HOLD FOR BTS, ONE THING REMAINS CERTAIN, WITH THE SUPPORT, DEVOTION AND LOYALTY OF A.R.M.Y, THE ONLY WAY IS UP!

BTS GLOSSARY

- ★ Aegyo
- ★ Akgae
- ★ All-kill – The name given to a newly released track that sweeps the South Korean music charts.
- ★ Bias - This refers to your favourite member of a K-Pop band.
- ★ Bonsang - Given at awards ceremonies to acknowledge outstanding music achievements.
- ★ Collaborations
- ★ Comeback
- ★ Daesang - The grand prize awarded at a K-Pop awards ceremony.
- ★ Fancafe
- ★ Fanchant
- ★ Fandom name
- ★ Fanmade content
- ★ Hallyu
- ★ Hwaiting
- ★ Instiz
- ★ Maknae
- ★ Mini album
- ★ MV
- ★ Noona
- ★ Nugu
- ★ Oppa
- ★ Oppalogist
- ★ Perfect All-Kill – The name given to a track that has an All-Kill and lands at number one on the Instiz Weekly Chart.
- ★ PV
- ★ Rookie
- ★ Sasaeng fans
- ★ Selca
- ★ Special stages
- ★ Stan
- ★ Subunits
- ★ Trainee
- ★ Visual

BIG QUIZ ANSWERS

- RM, Suga
- 2013
- Suga
- V and Jin
- RM
- J-Hope
- V
- 30th December 1995
- Wake Up: Open your Eyes
- Blood Sweat and Tears
- Wale
- Jungkook
- 2017
- BTS World Tour: Love Yourself
- Korean Wave
- Jungkook
- Adorable Representative MC for Youth
- Into the Magic Shop
- Wake Up
- N.O.

CROSSWORD ANSWERS

1. DNA
2. BANGTAN TV
3. ROOKIE KING
4. JIMIN
5. JUNGKOOK
6. WINGS
7. BIG HIT ENTERTAINMENT
8. JIN

DARK AND WILD

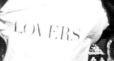